REMOTE
BUT NOT ALONE

Navigating the Challenges of Working from Home

By
DARREN MASONE

Copyright © DARREN MASONE

All rights reserved. No part of this guide may be reproduced in any form without permission in writing from the publisher except in the case of brief quotations embodied in critical articles or reviews.

Legal & Disclaimer

The information contained in this book and its contents is not designed to replace or take the place of any form of medical or professional advice; and is not meant to replace the need for independent medical, financial, legal or other professional advice or services, as may be required. The content and information in this book has been provided for educational and entertainment purposes only.

The content and information contained in this book has been compiled from sources deemed reliable, and it is accurate to the best of the Author's knowledge, information and belief. However, the Author cannot guarantee its accuracy and validity and cannot be held liable for any errors and/or omissions. Further, changes are periodically made to this book as and when needed. Where appropriate and/or necessary, you must consult a professional (including but not limited to your doctor, attorney, financial advisor or such other professional advisor) before using any of the suggested remedies, techniques, or information in this book.

Upon using the contents and information contained in this book, you agree to hold harmless the Author from and against any damages, costs, and expenses, including any legal fees potentially resulting from the application of any of the information provided by this book. This disclaimer applies to any loss, damages or injury caused by the use and application, whether directly or indirectly, of any advice or information presented, whether for breach of contract, tort, negligence, personal injury, criminal intent, or under any other cause of action.

You agree to accept all risks of using the information presented inside this book.

You agree that by continuing to read this book, where appropriate and/or necessary, you shall consult a professional (including but not limited to your doctor, attorney, or financial advisor or such other advisor as needed) before using any of the suggested remedies, techniques, or information in this book.

Table of Content

Introduction 7
Why You Need This Book? 7

Chapter 1... 11
Evolution of Remote Work (Or: How We Got Here).......................... 12
Remote Work Benefits vs. Drawbacks..................................... 14

Chapter 2 19
What Workplace Isolation Actually Means................................ 20
The Difference Between Solitude vs. Work Isolation (And Why It Matters).. 22
The Emotional & Professional Consequences of Remote Work: More Than Just Feeling Lonely 22

Chapter 3 27
The Connection Between Remote Work and Mental Health 27
Signs of Declining Well-being 28
The Loneliness-Burnout Link 29

Chapter 4 31
Home vs. Office: Different Distractions 31
How Multitasking Kills Productivity.................................... 32
Creating a Focused Workspace 33

Chapter 5 35
Common Virtual Miscommunications 35
Zoom Fatigue and Messaging Overload 36
Building Trust Without Face Time....................................... 36

Chapter 6 39
Why Remote Workers Overwork 39
The Danger of Being "Always On" 40
Time Management and Self-Discipline Strategies 40

Chapter 7 43
Team Synergy in a Digital World 43
Tools and Habits for Remote Collaboration 44
Encouraging Creativity from Afar 45

Chapter 8 47
Internet Reliability and Software Lags 47
Best Practices for a Smooth Tech Setup 48
Cybersecurity Basics for Remote Work 49

Chapter 9 51
Daily Routines That Strengthen Mental Toughness 51
Staying Socially Connected While Working Solo 52
Preventing Burnout Before It Starts 53

Chapter 10 55
Hybrid Models and Digital Nomadism 55
What Successful Remote Companies Do Differently 56
Creating a Sustainable Remote Work Lifestyle 57

Conclusion 59

References 60

Introduction

Imagine it's 2:47 PM on a Tuesday, and you're staring at your reflection in a black Zoom screen, wondering when you started looking so tired. Your kitchen table; sorry, "home office," is littered with coffee rings and sticky notes. You've just survived your fourth video call of the day, but during the presentation, the neighbor's dog barked loudly, and your toddler made a surprise appearance through the locked door. As you close your laptop, something unexpected hits you. Not relief but loneliness. Deep, aching, professional loneliness that makes zero sense because you've literally been talking to people all day.

If this is familiar, welcome to the club nobody wanted to join but 42% of the American workforce and the rest of the world now calls home. Let's face it, working from home sounded like a dream at first, right? Roll out of bed, grab your coffee, and start working in your pajamas. No commute, no dress code, and no annoying office politics. Sounds like a win on paper, but if you've been working remotely for a while now, you've probably realized there's more to it than just enjoying a slower morning routine.

If you've ever felt guilty for missing your annoying coworker's interruptions, or found yourself having full conversations with your delivery driver just to hear another human voice during work hours, you're not losing it. You're human. And you're definitely not alone in feeling alone. Then again, it doesn't have to be this way. You can absolutely thrive while working from home. The key is knowing how to manage the challenges, make your environment work for you, and prioritize your mental well-being. That's exactly what this book is about.

Why You Need This Book?

The thing that makes this book different from every other remote work guide gathering digital dust on your e-reader, is that we're not going to pretend this is easy or that positive thinking solves everything. Some days remote work genuinely sucks, and that's okay. What's not okay is suffering through it without the right tools and strategies.

If you've ever wondered if everyone else has figured out some remote work secret you missed. Trust me, they haven't. Even the people posting perfectly curated home office setups on LinkedIn are figuring it out as they go.

If you're the "successful" remote worker who looks great on paper but feels like you're slowly disappearing. Your productivity metrics are solid, your manager loves you, but you catch yourself staring out the window wondering if this is what career fulfillment is supposed to feel like. MIT research shows that remote workers often experience "career invisibility," being less likely to receive promotions or recognition. If this resonates, you need strategies for staying visible and engaged.

Perhaps you're the reluctant remote convert who got pushed into this lifestyle by circumstance. You miss the office energy, the spontaneous brainstorming sessions, even the terrible coffee. A Harvard Business School study found that forced remote workers show 38% higher stress levels than voluntary remote workers. If that's you, this book will help you find your footing.

If you are drowning in the deep end of newly remote work. Your productivity has tanked, your work-life boundaries have evaporated, and you're pretty sure your houseplants are judging your professional choices. According to Microsoft's Work Trend Index, 54% of remote workers feel overworked, and 39% are flat-out exhausted. If these numbers feel personal, we've got your back.

Maybe you're the hybrid worker playing a constant game of professional musical chairs. You're not fully remote or fully in-office, which somehow gives you the challenges of both and the benefits of neither. Research from Accenture shows hybrid workers often report feeling "caught between two worlds." Sound familiar?

You could be the manager trying to lead a team you can barely see. Your employees seem fine in meetings, but you suspect there's more going on beneath the surface. Google's Project Aristotle research shows that psychological safety; feeling safe to take risks and be vulnerable, is crucial for team performance, but it's harder to build virtually.

Or maybe you're just tired. Tired of pretending that working in sweatpants is the dream when some days it feels more like professional purgatory. Tired of hearing "you're so lucky you get to work from home" when you'd trade your kitchen table office for cubicle walls and fluorescent lighting in a heartbeat.

One thing nobody talks about is that you can love remote work and still struggle with it. You can be grateful for the flexibility and still miss human connection. You can be more productive than ever and still feel like something's missing. This book won't judge your complicated feelings about remote work. Instead, it'll help you manage them effectively.

By the time you finish this book, you won't just be surviving remote work; you'll be designing a version that actually fits your life, your personality, and your goals. Because the one secret that every successful remote workers knows is that it's not about adapting yourself to remote work; it's about adapting remote work to you. Are you ready to stop feeling like you're doing remote work wrong and start building a version that is genuinely right for you? Stay with me! Let's get right in.

Chapter 1
The New Normal

A few years ago, if you told someone that working from home would become the norm, they might have laughed. Remember when "working from home" meant you were either sick, waiting for the cable guy, or possibly slacking off? When the biggest remote work debate was whether you could wear pajama pants to a conference call (as long as nobody could see them)?

Those days feel like ancient history now, don't they? Now remote work is everywhere. It's no longer a quirky perk for freelancers or an occasional option for those lucky enough to land a "work-from-home" job. It's the standard. And for many of us, it feels like the world has flipped upside down. But this change didn't just happen overnight; this "new normal" has been in the making for a while.

In March 2020, the world's largest work-from-home experiment began; not by choice, but by necessity. Overnight, kitchen tables became boardrooms, bedroom corners turned into office spaces, and "you're on mute" became the most-spoken phrase in corporate world. What was supposed to be a temporary adjustment became the blueprint for how millions of us now spend our working lives. But here's the thing about overnight transformations: they rarely come with instruction manuals. One day you're grabbing coffee with colleagues between meetings, and the next you're trying to decode whether your boss's delayed email response means you're in trouble or they're just overwhelmed. Welcome to the new normal; a place where the rules are still being written and everyone's making it up as they go along.

Evolution of Remote Work (Or: How We Got Here)

Remote work is hardly a new concept. In fact, it's been around for decades in various forms, from telecommuting in the '90s to more modern freelance gigs. However, it was often seen as a rare exception rather than a widespread practice. Let's time travel for a moment. Remote work didn't start with Zoom calls and Slack notifications. It's been quietly evolving for decades, like that friend who gradually changes their style until one day you realize they look completely different.

Back in the 1970s, Jack Nilles coined the term "telecommuting" while working for NASA. His vision? Reducing traffic congestion and air pollution by letting people work from home one day a week. Revolutionary thinking for an era when computers were the size of refrigerators and "mobile phone" was an oxymoron.

The 1990s brought us dial-up internet and the radical idea that maybe, just maybe, some work didn't require a physical presence in a fluorescent-lit cubicle. Early remote work pioneers were often freelancers, consultants, or employees of progressive tech companies willing to experiment with "flexible arrangements."

By 2005, about 1.8 million Americans worked remotely. It was still considered alternative, slightly suspicious, and definitely not mainstream. Fast-forward to 2019, and that number had grown to 5.7 million; a significant jump, but still representing just 3.6% of the workforce.

How the Pandemic Accelerated the Evolution of Remote Work

The 2020 covid-19 pandemic changed everything when the world suddenly shut down in the earliest months of the year. Businesses had no choice but to adapt, or risk shutting their doors for good. Remote work wasn't just an option; it was the only option. In a matter of weeks, companies across the globe had to embrace digital communication and remote collaboration, whether they were ready or not.

The change was massive. According to a McKinsey report, the pandemic accelerated the adoption of remote work by several years in just a matter of months. For instance, while only 24% of U.S. employees worked remotely before the pandemic, that number shot up to 42% by mid-2020. This dramatic change was no longer just a response to a crisis; it was a full-on, long-term shift in the way we work.

Global Workplace Analytics reported that remote work grew by 159% between 2005 and 2017. Impressive, right? Well, hold onto your ergonomic desk chair because in 2020 alone, remote work increased by 2,000%. Not a typo. Two thousand percent.

We went from 5% of the workforce being fully remote to 42% practically overnight. That's like going from knowing five people who are vegetarian to having nearly half your friends give up meat simultaneously. The scale and speed of this shift is unprecedented in modern work history.

When the World Stopped Commuting?

March 13, 2020. Remember that Friday? For many of us, it was the last "normal" day at the office. The day we grabbed our laptops "just in case" we needed to work from home for a week or two. Some people didn't even take their desk plants home. Those plants became unwitting symbols of how wrong we all were about the timeline.

What happened next was the largest workplace experiment in human history, conducted without control groups, preparation time, or informed consent. According to Stanford economist Nicholas Bloom, we compressed 10 years of remote work evolution into 10 weeks.

The numbers tell an incredible story. Before the pandemic, Zoom was handling 10 million daily meeting participants. By April 2020? Three hundred million. Microsoft Teams saw a 1,000% increase in usage within a single month. Your Wi-Fi router, meanwhile, was probably crying for mercy. But the real transformation wasn't technological, it was psychological and cultural. Suddenly, seeing someone's kid interrupt a meeting wasn't unprofessional; it was relatable. Pets became unofficial meeting mascots. The phrase "sorry, construction noise" entered the corporate lexicon alongside "quarterly projections" and "synergistic solutions."

Companies that had spent years debating whether employees could work from home one day a week were suddenly discovering their entire operations could function remotely. IBM, which had famously ended its remote work program in 2017, found itself with 95% of its workforce operating from home. The transformation wasn't just about where we worked, it changed how we thought about work itself. According to a Gartner survey, 88% of organizations worldwide made it mandatory or encouraged employees to work from home. This wasn't just changing jobs; it was reshaping the fundamental relationship between work and life.

Remote Work Benefits vs. Drawbacks

Of course, as with anything, remote work comes with its own mix of pros and cons. Read on to find out.

The Bright Side: Why Remote Work Can Be Amazing

Let's start with the obvious wins because, despite the challenges we've explored throughout this book, remote work genuinely offers some incredible benefits. After living through this transition, we now have real data to back up what were once just hopeful theories. Here's why remote work can be amazing:

1. Saving Time from Less Commuting

The average American spends 54 minutes commuting each day. That's 220 hours a year; nearly six full work weeks, spent sitting in traffic or crammed into public transportation. Remote workers got those hours back. Many invested them in sleep, exercise, family time, or picking up hobbies they'd long forgotten. A Harvard Business School study found that eliminating the commute alone improved work-life balance for 71% of remote workers. And it doesn't just stop at time savings. According to the Texas A&M Transportation Institute, the average commuter burns 54 gallons of gas yearly just getting to work. Remote workers? Zero gallons, zero road rage, and zero "sorry I'm late, there was an accident on I-95" excuses.

2. Improved Productivity

Here's where it gets interesting. Remember all those concerns about employees slacking off at home? Stanford's work-from-home experiment with Chinese travel company Ctrip showed a 13% productivity increase among remote workers. How? Fewer sick days, fewer breaks, and of course, more time to work due to the absence of the commute. But it's not just about working more hours, it's about working better hours. Remote workers reported tackling their most challenging tasks during their peak performance times, rather than being forced into a rigid 9-to-5 schedule.

3. The Flexibility Factor

Remote work offers something incredibly valuable, but hard to quantify: flexibility. Not just the ability to wear pajama pants (though that's nice) but the flexibility to handle life's curveballs without derailing your career. Need to be home for a repair person? No problem. Want to attend your kid's school play at 2 PM? Done. Have a doctor's appointment? Easily managed. This flexibility is particularly valuable for caregivers, people with disabilities, and anyone whose life doesn't fit into traditional office hours. Research from FlexJobs shows that 97% of remote workers would recommend remote work to others, with flexibility being the top reason. When employees have more control over their schedules, they report higher job satisfaction and lower stress levels.

4. The Talent Pool Revolution

For employers, remote work broke down geographical barriers. Suddenly, a company in Ohio could hire the perfect candidate in Oregon, without requiring relocation. It opened up opportunities for both employers seeking specialized talent and employees who didn't want to move to expensive cities. Harvard Business School found that job postings for remote positions receive 2.5 times more applications than location-specific roles. This expanded talent pool benefits everyone: companies get better candidates, and workers access opportunities that might have otherwise required major life changes.

The Dark Side: When Remote Work Gets Complicated

Let's be real, if remote work were purely sunshine and productivity gains, you probably wouldn't be reading this book. The challenges are real, significant, and often unexpected. Let's talk about the "shadow side" of remote work:

1. The Loneliness Epidemic

Humans are social creatures, and work provides more social interaction than we realize until it's gone. The casual conversations, the brainstorming sessions, and even the grumbling about the broken coffee machine create social bonds that are hard to replicate virtually. Buffer's State of Remote Work report found loneliness to be one of the top challenges, affecting 21% of remote workers in 2023. This isn't just about missing office parties, it's professional isolation that can impact career development, mental health, and job satisfaction.

2. The Boundaries That Disappeared

When your office is at home, turning off work becomes much more complicated. There's no physical transition, no leaving the building to signal the end of the workday. Your laptop is always there, silently suggesting you check one more email. Research from NordLayer shows remote employees work an average of 2.5 extra hours per day compared to office workers. That's essentially adding a part-time job to a full-time one without even realizing it.

3. Communication in Translation

Remember when you could "read the room"? When you could tell if your joke landed or if someone was confused by their facial expression? Digital communication strips away many of those non-verbal cues. A Microsoft study found that remote teams become more siloed, communicating less with people outside their immediate team. This can result in missed collaboration opportunities and hinder innovation.

4. The Technology Trap

Working remotely means relying on technology that's often beyond your control. Internet outages, software glitches, and the dreaded "can you hear me now?" moments can derail meetings and damage professional relationships. A survey by Upwork found 22% of remote workers struggle with unreliable internet, while 18% face difficulties accessing necessary tools and software. When your office is digital, technical problems can quickly become career problems.

The Verdict? It's Complicated! So, where does this leave us? Is remote work the future of employment, or a necessary evil we're all learning to tolerate? The answer, like most things, is: it depends. Research from PwC's Remote Work Survey found that 83% of employers say remote work has been successful for their company, while 77% of remote workers wanted to continue working remotely at least one day per week after the pandemic. These are promising numbers, but they don't tell the whole story. While the future of remote work looks bright for many, it's not without its complications.

Remote work isn't one-size-fits-all. For some, it's the ultimate dream; flexible, productive, and freeing. For others, it's a complicated balancing act of isolation, blurred boundaries, and tech glitches. The key insight? Remote work isn't inherently good or bad, it's a tool that works brilliantly for some people and situations while creating challenges for others. Success depends largely on how well you understand both the opportunities and the pitfalls, and how effectively you can navigate them.

Throughout the rest of this book, we'll explore practical strategies for maximizing the benefits while minimizing the drawbacks. Because the new normal isn't going anywhere, but that doesn't mean you have to simply endure it. You can actually make it work for you.

Chapter 2
Understanding Remote Work Isolation

At first, the idea of working from home might have sounded like just the life to live; no more awkward small talk by the coffee machine, no more noisy cubicles, and a chance to work in peace. But as time goes on, the reality of remote work starts to settle in. One feeling that creeps up on many remote workers is a sense of isolation, and it hits you at the strangest moments.

Maybe it's 5 PM on a Thursday, and you realize the only voice you've heard all day is your own; answering emails out loud to break the silence. Or perhaps it's during a team meeting when everyone's laughing at a joke, but you're watching it happen through a screen, feeling like you're observing a party you can't quite join.

You are not alone, Jennifer, a marketing manager from Seattle, found herself having a full conversation with her Uber Eats delivery driver just to experience what she called "organic human interaction." Not scheduled, not agenda-driven, not through a screen; just two people talking about the weather because it felt like a luxury she'd forgotten existed.

This is workplace isolation, and it's become the elephant in the room that nobody wants to talk about in team meetings. Because how do you explain to your boss that you feel lonely when you're technically surrounded by colleagues all day? How do you articulate that professional isolation when your calendar is packed with video calls?

Here's the thing about isolation in remote work: it's not what you think it is, and it's definitely not what anyone prepared us for. At first, it may feel like a bit of quiet time to focus, but over weeks and months, that silence can become overwhelming. It's easy to feel like you're missing out, like you've been left behind in a world that keeps moving; while you stay still, alone in front of your screen.

So, what's really going on when we talk about isolation in the remote work world? It's more than just being physically alone. It's a deeper, more emotional experience that can affect your mental health and productivity. Let's take a closer look.

What Workplace Isolation Actually Means

Workplace isolation refers to the emotional and social distance between you and your colleagues, a distance that's amplified when you're working remotely. It's that sense of being cut off from the world, even when you're technically still part of a team. The lack of face-to-face interaction can lead to feelings of disconnection, as if you're just a "name on a screen" rather than a valued team member.

For some, this isolation can feel like being on the outside looking in. It's not just about the physical absence from coworkers, but the absence of spontaneous interactions; those quick chats in the hallway, casual lunch breaks, or even the chance to overhear a conversation that sparks new ideas. Without these organic moments, remote workers may begin to feel disconnected and left out of the team's culture.

When researchers talk about workplace isolation, they're not describing the person who hides in their cubicle avoiding small talk. They're talking about something much more complex and, frankly, more common than most of us realize.

Dr. Sarah Doyle from the University of Connecticut defines workplace isolation as *"the psychological state where an employee feels disconnected from their work environment, colleagues, and organizational culture."* Notice that word; feels. You can be surrounded by people (or video calls) and still experience profound workplace isolation.

In traditional offices, isolation might look like being excluded from lunch groups or not being invited to informal meetings. But remote work isolation? It's sneakier. It's the gradual realization that you're missing context other people seem to have. It's wondering if your teammates are having conversations you're not part of. It's the growing sense that everyone else got a memo you didn't receive.

Research from Virtira Consulting found that 43% of remote workers feel isolated at least once a week, with 21% feeling isolated daily. But here's the kicker: many of these workers didn't even recognize what they were feeling as isolation until it was specifically named for them.

The Basics of Remote Isolation

Remote work isolation typically shows up in four distinct ways, and you might recognize yourself in one or more of these patterns:

1. Informational Isolation: You feel out of the loop. Office conversations that used to happen naturally; updates about projects, changes in direction, office politics, even who's hiring or who's leaving, now happen without you. You find yourself piecing together information from scattered clues rather than being naturally included in the flow.

2. Social Isolation: The relationships that made work enjoyable have become transactional. Your interactions with colleagues are limited to project-specific conversations. You miss the birthday celebrations, the complaining about bad coffee, the casual "how was your weekend?" exchanges that build genuine connections.

3. Physical Isolation: Your world has shrunk to your home office space. You miss the energy of a busy workplace, the background hum of productivity, even the minor inconveniences that reminded you that you were part of something larger than yourself.

4. Emotional Isolation: This is perhaps the most challenging, as you may feel like you're managing your work emotions alone. There's no one to vent to about a frustrating client call, no colleague to share excitement about a project win, no immediate support when you're having a tough day.

The Difference Between Solitude vs. Work Isolation (And Why It Matters)

This is where it gets interesting: solitude and isolation aren't the same thing, even though they often feel identical when you're living through them. Solitude is chosen. It's the peaceful quiet when you can focus deeply on a project without interruption. It's the satisfaction of controlling your environment and energy. It's what many of us thought we wanted when we dreamed about working from home.

Isolation, on the other hand, is imposed. It's the feeling of being cut off even when you don't want to be. It's the sense that connection is available to others but somehow not to you. Dr. Heather Hansen from Boston University explains it this way: "*Solitude energizes, while isolation depletes. Solitude feels like a choice, while isolation feels like a sentence.*"

The tricky part? You can experience both in the same day, sometimes within the same hour. You might love the solitude of your morning deep work session, then feel isolated during a team meeting where everyone seems more connected to each other than to you.

The Emotional & Professional Consequences of Remote Work: More Than Just Feeling Lonely

Let's address the elephant in the room: workplace isolation isn't just about feeling a little lonely or missing office snacks. The emotional impact is real, measurable, and affects both personal well-being and professional performance.

One of the most surprising consequences of workplace isolation is its impact on professional confidence. Dr. Amy Edmondson's research on psychological safety at Harvard Business School reveals that isolated workers are 67% less likely to speak up with ideas or concerns during meetings.

Think about it: in an office, you get constant micro-feedback. A nod during a presentation, a colleague asking follow-up questions after a meeting, someone building on your idea in real-time. These small interactions continuously calibrate your sense of professional competence. Remote workers often miss these confidence-building moments. Without regular informal feedback, you might start second-guessing contributions that would have felt natural in person. Ivanka, a software developer from Austin, described it perfectly: *"I used to know when I had a good idea because people would lean in or start nodding. Now I throw ideas into the Zoom void and hope for the best."*

Isolation can also amplify imposter syndrome, that feeling that you're not qualified for your role and everyone's about to figure it out. When you're not seeing colleagues struggle with similar challenges or make similar mistakes, it's easy to assume everyone else has it figured out while you're barely keeping up. Research from the International Journal of Behavioral Science found that remote workers report 23% higher levels of imposter syndrome compared to their office-based counterparts. The lack of casual conversations where colleagues might mention their own challenges or uncertainties leaves remote workers feeling like they're the only ones who don't have everything under control.

Working in isolation also increases decision fatigue. In an office, many small decisions get made collectively or through casual conversations. *"Should we push back this deadline?"* becomes a quick hallway conversation. *"Is this email tone appropriate?"* gets answered with a quick *"hey, can you read this before I send it?"*

Remote workers often carry the cognitive load of these decisions alone, which can be mentally exhausting. Dr. Roy Baumeister's research on decision fatigue shows that making decisions in isolation requires more mental energy than collaborative decision-making, leading to faster cognitive depletion throughout the day.

The Professional Consequences: Career Impact You Didn't See Coming

The professional stakes of workplace isolation extend far beyond feeling disconnected. They can impact career trajectory in ways that aren't immediately obvious but compound over time.

"*Out of sight, out of mind*" isn't just a saying, it's a career reality for many remote workers. Research from Harvard Business Review found that remote employees are promoted 31% less frequently than their in-office counterparts, even when performance metrics are identical. This isn't necessarily due to conscious bias. It's often about informal influence and visibility. The quick hallway conversation that leads to being included in a new project, the impromptu brainstorming session that showcases your creativity, the casual lunch where you learn about upcoming opportunities, these moments are harder to recreate virtually.

Professional development often happens through informal mentorship; senior colleagues who take interest in your growth, offer advice, and create opportunities. These relationships typically develop through casual interactions and shared experiences that are challenging to replicate in remote settings. A study by Deloitte found that remote workers are 38% less likely to have informal mentorship relationships compared to office-based employees. This mentorship gap can slow career development and reduce access to internal opportunities and professional guidance.

How about the innovation isolation? Some of the most innovative work happens through unplanned collaboration; the conversation that sparks a new idea, the colleague who overhears your challenge and offers a solution, the cross-departmental insights that emerge from casual interactions. MIT research on innovation patterns shows that breakthrough ideas are 65% more likely to emerge from informal, cross-functional interactions rather than scheduled meetings. Remote workers, particularly those experiencing isolation, have fewer opportunities for these serendipitous innovative moments.

Throughout the rest of this book, we'll explore specific strategies for building connection, maintaining visibility, and creating the professional relationships that make work fulfilling. But first, let's understand how isolation intersects with mental health because the two are more connected than most people realize. The key insight to carry forward? Workplace isolation isn't a character flaw or a sign that you're not cut out for remote work. It's a predictable challenge with practical solutions.

And the first step toward solving it is understanding exactly what you're dealing with. Now that we've named it, we can tame it.

Chapter 3
The Mental Health Equation

We often talk about work-life balance, and how to juggle our professional responsibilities with our personal lives. But when your *"work"* and *"life"* are taking place in the same place, that balance becomes more like a blurred line. Remote work isn't just about getting your tasks done without commuting; it's about managing your mental health while you do it. After all, your mind plays a major role in how you show up to work each day; physically, emotionally, and even professionally.

The Connection Between Remote Work and Mental Health

If you've been working remotely for any length of time, you might have noticed something: the longer you stay away from an office setting, the more your mental health can start to change. It's subtle at first, maybe you feel a bit more tired or irritable, or you notice that your motivation has slipped. But over time, the effects of isolation, lack of routine, and blurred boundaries between work and personal life can add up, leading to anxiety, stress, and even depression.

Dr. Ellen Selkie from the University of Michigan has been studying the mental health impacts of remote work since before the pandemic. Her research reveals something counterintuitive: the people who seem most successful at remote work are often the ones struggling most with its mental health challenges.

"High achievers and self-motivated individuals initially thrive in remote environments," Dr. Selkie explains. *"But they're also most likely to develop problematic patterns because they lack external boundaries and social accountability that previously regulated their work behavior."*

Here's the data that might surprise you: according to the American Psychological Association's 2023 Work and Well-being Survey, remote workers report 18% higher levels of stress than office workers, despite having greater flexibility. They also show 22% higher rates of anxiety and 15% higher rates of depression. But here's the twist; these same remote workers also report higher job satisfaction and better work-life integration. How is this possible? Call it the mental health paradox of our time.

Working from home, without those moments, can feel like you're constantly in your own head, disconnected from others. In fact, a study by Buffer found that mental health is one of the top struggles for remote workers, with 32% of respondents listing it as their biggest challenge. That's not surprising considering how much remote work can alter your daily routine and how little you might have to "look forward to" outside of work.

Signs of Declining Well-being

The signs of mental health struggles when working remotely can be hard to spot, especially since they sneak up on you over time. However, they're definitely there, often manifesting in both physical and emotional ways. Here are some signs that your mental health might be in decline:

1. Chronic Fatigue: This is not the *"I stayed up too late"* kind of tired, but a deep, ongoing exhaustion that doesn't seem to improve with rest. Remote work can lead to burnout, especially if you're struggling to find a clear distinction between work time and personal time.

2. Increased Irritability: If you're snapping at family members, colleagues, or even strangers during your daily routine, it could be a sign that your emotional reserves are running low. Stress, loneliness, and the lack of physical social interaction can all contribute to mood swings and frustration.

3. Loss of Motivation: One of the most noticeable signs of mental strain is the feeling of being "*stuck*." If you're no longer excited about your work, find it hard to focus, or feel a sense of dread when starting your day, it could be due to a deeper mental health issue triggered by remote work.

4. Physical Symptoms: Mental health isn't just in your head, it's also in your body. Headaches, trouble sleeping, back pain from poor posture, and stomach issues can all be signs that your mental health is suffering.

If you notice any of these symptoms, it's time to take a step back and assess how your remote work situation is affecting you. Mental health is as important as physical health, and if left unchecked, the consequences can be severe.

The Loneliness-Burnout Link

Here's where things get tricky. The feeling of loneliness, which often comes with remote work, is not just a passing phase. It can lead directly to burnout; a state of physical, emotional, and mental exhaustion caused by prolonged stress.

You might be surprised by how deeply loneliness can affect your work performance. When you're isolated, it's easier to get distracted, procrastinate, or feel unmotivated. A lack of social support can lead to self-doubt and anxiety, which only compounds the stress you're already feeling. And over time, if those feelings aren't addressed, they can turn into full-blown burnout.

Studies show that loneliness and burnout go hand-in-hand. Harvard Business Review cites research that found employees who experience social isolation are at a much higher risk for burnout, nearly 60% more likely, in fact. In other words, when you feel disconnected from your coworkers and friends, it becomes harder to stay engaged, stay productive, and, ultimately, stay healthy. But burnout isn't inevitable. Recognizing the signs of mental distress early on is key. In the chapters ahead, we'll explore ways to tackle loneliness, establish healthy routines, and create work environments that promote mental well-being.

Chapter 4
Distraction Nation

Let's be real, working from home can be a battle for focus. When you're not sitting in an office surrounded by colleagues and deadlines, the distractions at home seem to multiply. The laundry piles up. The dog needs walking. The refrigerator keeps calling your name. You might start your day with good intentions, but by noon, you've somehow watched two episodes of your favorite show, scrolled through social media, and forgotten to send that important email.

It's a common struggle for remote workers, and it's easy to see why. Without the structure and environment of an office, staying focused can feel like an uphill battle. But distractions aren't just about willpower, they're about understanding the types of distractions that exist in your environment and how to manage them. Let's examine the most common distractions at home, the myth of multitasking, and how you can create a workspace that helps you thrive.

Home vs. Office: Different Distractions

In an office setting, distractions are usually predictable; chatty coworkers, the occasional meeting, or the printer that always jams at the wrong time. But at home, distractions are a whole different animal. They're personal, constant, and often irresistible. The first major difference is that you're in your personal space. You're surrounded by the very things that you associate with relaxation and comfort: the couch, the TV, the kitchen, the bed. It's tempting to sneak in a quick break, but those "*quick*" breaks can quickly add up to hours of unproductive time. Then there's the issue of household chores. Maybe you see that pile of dishes in the sink or a laundry basket overflowing with clothes. It's hard to stay focused when you know your house isn't in tip-top shape. You might even think, "*I'll just get this done, and then I'll focus,*" only to find that a 10-minute chore turns into a 45-minute detour.

Family and pets also come into play. Kids, roommates, or even just the need to take care of a pet can create interruptions you wouldn't face in a traditional office. A simple knock on the door or a phone call from a loved one can break your focus, sometimes for hours. According to a Harvard Business Review study, 51% of remote workers say that their biggest challenge is the difficulty of managing distractions from family members.

In the office, there's usually a structure that helps minimize distractions; people are focused on their tasks, and there are clearer boundaries between work and personal life. At home, that structure can be harder to establish.

How Multitasking Kills Productivity

You've probably heard it a thousand times: "*Multitasking is the key to productivity!*" It sounds great in theory, but in reality, multitasking can actually reduce productivity by up to 40%, according to a study from Stanford University.

When you try to do multiple things at once, whether it's answering emails, writing a report, or checking social media while on a work call, you're not really focusing on any one task. Your brain is rapidly switching between different tasks, and that constant shifting lowers your efficiency. You might feel like you're accomplishing more, but studies show that multitasking actually leads to more mistakes, slower work, and greater mental fatigue.

Here's why: Our brains aren't designed to focus on more than one complex task at a time. When we multitask, we put more strain on our cognitive resources, which slows us down. The result? Tasks take longer, mistakes increase, and your stress levels go up.

Creating a Focused Workspace

Now that we've talked about the distractions, let's talk about solutions. The key to improving your focus and productivity while working from home is to design a workspace that's tailored to your needs; one that minimizes distractions and promotes deep focus. To do this:

1. Designate a Space: One of the biggest challenges of remote work is that your home is your office. To reduce distractions, it's important to create a physical boundary between your personal space and your workspace. Ideally, find a room or corner that's dedicated to work, so you can "*leave*" your office at the end of the day.

2. Declutter Your Space: Clutter can be overwhelming and distracting. Studies show that a tidy workspace leads to clearer thinking and better productivity. Try to keep your desk clear of non-work-related items, especially those little distractions like a half-finished puzzle or your favorite book.

3. Set Boundaries: This is crucial, especially if you live with others. Communicate with family or roommates about your work hours and the importance of minimizing interruptions. Consider using headphones or noise-canceling technology if necessary.

4. Use Technology Wisely: There's no shortage of tools to help you stay focused. Apps like Forest, Focus@Will, or Pomodoro timers can help keep you on track by limiting your time on distracting apps or websites. Another effective strategy is turning off non-essential notifications on your phone and computer while you work.

5. Take Regular Breaks: You might think that powering through without breaks will make you more productive, but research shows that the opposite is true. Taking short breaks throughout the day improves focus and mental clarity. Step outside, grab a coffee, or do some light stretching, whatever helps you recharge.

In the end, the goal is to create an environment that supports your focus, reduces distractions, and boosts your productivity. With the right setup, you'll be able to stay on task and make the most of your time working from home.

Chapter 5
Communication Gaps and Digital Misfires

In this chapter, we'll talk about the communication challenges that come with remote work, from digital misfires to the emotional toll of virtual interactions. We'll also explore how you can bridge these gaps to ensure your messages land as intended and that your team remains connected, no matter the distance.

Common Virtual Miscommunications

When you're working remotely, you don't have the benefit of seeing someone's body language or hearing the tone of their voice in real-time. As a result, emails and messages can easily be misinterpreted. A simple "Sure!" can seem enthusiastic in person, but online, it might come across as curt. A well-intended joke might fall flat, or a question you thought was clear could be met with confusion.

One of the biggest culprits of virtual miscommunication is lack of context. In face-to-face interactions, we can rely on non-verbal cues, like a smile, a gesture, or the pacing of the conversation, to fill in the gaps. But without these cues, we're left to guess the meaning behind a message. Research by HubSpot found that 70% of people have experienced communication breakdowns in remote settings, often due to a lack of clear context.

Additionally, tone is notoriously difficult to convey online. A Forbes article reported that 90% of communication is non-verbal, which means that when we only have text or a few pixels on a screen to communicate, the chances of misunderstanding go up significantly. For instance, sarcasm can easily be taken literally in a text message, and humor doesn't always translate well on a Zoom call.

Zoom Fatigue and Messaging Overload

Raise your hand if you've ever found yourself staring at a Zoom screen, your mind wandering, wishing for a break. Zoom fatigue is real, and it's not just a passing inconvenience. Video calls are mentally draining for a few reasons. First, they require more focus than in-person conversations because you're trying to read facial expressions, tone, and body language; all while staring at a screen that may or may not be lagging. It's like trying to hold multiple conversations at once with limited energy.

Zoom fatigue has become a term in the remote work lexicon, and it's affecting people in a big way. A study by Stanford found that participants in video meetings experienced more fatigue than those in face-to-face ones. Part of it is the constant eye contact; when you're on a video call, you feel like you're always being watched. Additionally, the mental load of interpreting virtual cues and managing the technology can make video calls feel exhausting, especially when they're back-to-back.

However, it's not just video calls. Messaging overload can create its own set of problems. With email, Slack, WhatsApp, and a dozen other platforms, it can feel like your inbox is never empty. Trying to keep up with an avalanche of messages, while managing multiple tasks, is a surefire way to burn out. In fact, a Harvard Business Review survey found that remote workers often spend more time on digital communication tools than they did when they worked in an office—leading to an increase in stress and communication mishaps.

Building Trust Without Face Time

One of the hardest things about remote work is maintaining trust with your colleagues and clients without the benefit of casual, face-to-face interactions. Trust is built on those small, everyday moments, like the nod of approval in a meeting, a handshake after closing a deal, or a shared laugh during a coffee break. Without these, it can feel like you're constantly trying to prove yourself and your work.

Building trust remotely requires intentionality. One of the most important things is transparency. In the office, you might just pop into a coworker's office to discuss something, but remotely, it's essential to keep everyone in the loop. Regular check-ins, clear communication, and sharing progress updates can all help foster a sense of trust among team members.

Another key is consistency. When your team can rely on you to show up on time, meet deadlines, and communicate clearly, that trust starts to build. It might take a little more effort than it would in person, but it's absolutely possible to maintain strong relationships and a sense of camaraderie, even when you're miles apart.

Remember that active listening plays a huge role in building trust. When you're on a video call or chatting online, make sure you're really paying attention. Don't just respond, engage with what the other person is saying. Ask questions, offer feedback, and show that you value their input. These small acts can make a huge difference in building connection and trust within your remote team.

Chapter 6
Work-Life Boundary Blur

In this chapter, we'll dig into why remote workers tend to overwork, the dangers of being "always on," and how to build time management and self-discipline strategies that actually help you reclaim your personal time.

Why Remote Workers Overwork

It sounds counterintuitive, right? You're at home, which should mean you have more time to relax, take breaks, and enjoy life outside of work. But for many remote workers, the opposite is true. In fact, studies show that remote employees tend to work longer hours than their office-bound counterparts. According to a Buffer State of Remote Work report, 32% of remote workers struggle to disconnect after work hours, and 25% report that they work longer hours than they would in the office.

So, why does this happen? For starters, there's a mental shift when you work from home. When your office is just a few feet away from your couch or kitchen table, it's easy to think, "*I'll just get this one last thing done,*" even when it's late at night or during your weekend. There's a persistent pressure to always be available, to respond to emails in real-time, and to "*keep busy*" even when you've already put in a full day's work.

Another reason is the blurred boundaries between work and personal life. Without the structure of a traditional office, remote workers can struggle to create clear boundaries around when the workday starts and ends. You might not have a colleague reminding you to take a lunch break or a boss walking by to signal the end of your day. And let's not forget the emotional aspect of working remotely; if you're feeling disconnected or lonely, you might dive into work as a way to fill that gap, even if it's at the expense of your well-being.

The Danger of Being "Always On"

In today's digital world, being "*always on*" is more of a curse than a blessing. You're constantly tethered to your devices; checking emails, Slack messages, and calendar notifications, and it can feel like your work is never truly over. In fact, the sense of needing to be available at all times can lead to burnout.

A study by Deloitte found that 56% of remote workers feel "*always on,*" and 35% report feeling stressed out about being available at all times. This always-on mentality can lead to what experts call "*technostress,*" the stress of being continuously connected to work and technology. While technology makes it easier to collaborate remotely, it also makes it harder to disconnect. The idea of always being "on" can feel like you're constantly on the clock, even when you're not actively working. This can negatively impact your mental health, leaving you feeling drained, overwhelmed, and disconnected from your personal life.

It's important to recognize that being always available doesn't mean you're more productive; it means you're likely burning out. If you're constantly working without taking proper breaks, your efficiency, creativity, and well-being will suffer. The result? A decrease in both work quality and job satisfaction.

Time Management and Self-Discipline Strategies

Now that we've covered the reasons why remote workers overwork and the dangers of always being "on," let's talk about how to avoid burnout and create better boundaries between your work and personal life.

Effective time management and self-discipline are key to making remote work sustainable in the long run. Therefore:

1. Set Clear Work Hours: Treat your remote work like any other job; create a set schedule for when you're working and when you're off. Set a time to start your day and, just as importantly, a time to end it. Having a fixed work schedule can help you avoid the temptation to work late into the night or check your emails during weekends.

2. Establish a Dedicated Workspace: One of the easiest ways to create work-life separation is by designating a specific area for work. This will help your brain associate that space with productivity and focus. When the workday ends, physically leave that space to signal to your brain that it's time to switch off.

3. Use Time-Blocking: This method is all about assigning specific blocks of time to different tasks throughout the day. By setting aside time for focused work, meetings, and personal breaks, you can keep track of how you're spending your day. This strategy helps you stay disciplined and prevents you from feeling like you're always in work mode.

4. Set Boundaries with Technology: It's essential to turn off notifications or put your phone on "**Do Not Disturb**" when you're off the clock. Consider setting up a work profile on your devices so that when you're not working, you don't get distracted by work-related apps or emails.

5. Prioritize Breaks: Don't skip your breaks, especially when you're working from home. Taking regular breaks throughout the day has been shown to improve focus and productivity. Use your breaks to stretch, walk around, or even take a power nap.

6. Learn to Say No: Remote workers often feel compelled to take on every task that comes their way, thinking they can handle it all. But overextending yourself can quickly lead to burnout. It's okay to say no or delegate tasks when necessary. Prioritizing your time will help you focus on what's most important and avoid feeling overwhelmed.

In the end, finding the right balance between work and personal life is all about setting boundaries, being mindful of your mental health, and respecting your need for time off. When you establish clear work hours, create a structured environment, and prioritize self-care, remote work can be both productive and sustainable.

Chapter 7
Collaboration Without Walls

Gone are the days of spontaneous brainstorming sessions by the whiteboard or impromptu team huddles in the breakroom. When you're working remotely, collaboration looks a little different. There are no more casual conversations that spark great ideas, no one-to-one meetings where you can bounce thoughts off each other in real-time. Instead, you're relying on digital tools and planned virtual meetings to keep the ideas flowing. But don't worry; collaboration without walls is not only possible, it's necessary for building strong, creative, and connected teams. In this chapter, we'll explore how to keep the synergy alive in a digital workspace, the tools and habits that make remote collaboration effective, and how to encourage creativity when you're not all in the same room.

Team Synergy in a Digital World

In the traditional office, team synergy often happens naturally. The physical proximity creates opportunities for spontaneous interactions: the casual chat that sparks an idea, the quick meeting that solves a problem, or just being able to pop into someone's office for a minute to ask a question. In a remote world, however, creating synergy requires a little more effort. So, how do we maintain the energy and collaboration of an in-person team when everyone is scattered across different locations? It's all about intentionality. When you're not bumping into your colleagues in the hallway, you have to make time to connect. Regular virtual meetings, whether they're one-on-ones or team-wide check-ins, can help maintain that sense of community and keep everyone on the same page.

According to a Harvard Business Review study, remote teams that communicate regularly have higher levels of trust and better overall performance. But it's not just about the meetings, it's about fostering an environment where people feel comfortable sharing ideas. Building trust virtually takes work, but it's possible. Be sure to make space for open, honest conversations where everyone feels heard. Give team members opportunities to share feedback, celebrate small wins, and voice concerns. This kind of transparency builds a strong foundation of trust and collaboration.

Tools and Habits for Remote Collaboration

The right tools can make or break remote collaboration. The key is finding tools that not only allow you to communicate effectively, but also foster creativity, organization, and innovation. Try:

1. Project Management Tools: Platforms like Trello, Asana, or Monday.com help organize tasks, track progress, and keep everyone on the same page. These tools allow team members to collaborate in real-time, set deadlines, and visualize work in a way that's easy to follow, no matter where everyone is located.

2. Instant Messaging Platforms: Tools like Slack, Microsoft Teams, and Google Chat make quick communication easy and efficient. These platforms reduce the back-and-forth of email and allow for faster decision-making. They also offer spaces for team bonding, creating channels for non-work-related conversations (e.g., a #coffee-break or #weekend-plans channel) can help keep the human connection alive.

3. Video Conferencing: While Zoom, Google Meet, and Microsoft Teams allow for face-to-face interaction, it's important to use them wisely. Try mixing up your meeting formats to keep things fresh; use video calls for brainstorming sessions, one-on-ones, or social "watercooler" chats, but stick to messaging or project management tools for routine updates or short check-ins.

4. Collaborative Document Platforms: Tools like Google Docs, Miro, and Notion allow for real-time document editing, brainstorming, and sharing. These platforms are perfect for creating shared spaces where ideas can be jotted down and built upon by the entire team. Whether it's drafting a proposal or mapping out a project plan, collaborative documents make it easy to get input from everyone, no matter where they are.

5. Creative Tools: For remote teams to remain innovative, creative tools are essential. Software like Canva, Adobe Creative Cloud, and Figma allow for collaborative design work, giving teams the ability to work on graphics, web designs, or other creative projects together in real time.

Once you have the tools in place, it's all about building habits that support collaboration. Establish regular check-ins or brainstorming sessions, set aside time for creative thinking, and make sure there's always space for feedback.

Encouraging Creativity from Afar

When you're working remotely, it's easy to get stuck in a routine; your workday becomes a blur of tasks, meetings, and deadlines. But creativity doesn't thrive in a vacuum; it needs to be nurtured and encouraged. So how can you encourage creativity when your team isn't all in the same room? Thus:

1. Create a Safe Space for Ideas: In a remote environment, people may feel reluctant to speak up or share ideas, especially if they're not sure how their input will be received. Make sure your team knows that their ideas are valued, no matter how big or small. Encourage brainstorming sessions where no idea is off-limits, and create an environment where experimentation is welcomed.

2. Make Time for "Unstructured" Conversations: Some of the best ideas come from casual, unplanned conversations. Try scheduling "*creative*" sessions with no agenda, just a time for team members to share whatever's on their minds. You'd be surprised what emerges when people are given the freedom to speak openly.

3. Foster Cross-Disciplinary Collaboration: Remote work can sometimes isolate people in their specific roles, but creativity thrives when people from different backgrounds come together to solve problems. Encourage team members from different departments or areas of expertise to collaborate on projects. The mixing of perspectives often leads to fresh, innovative ideas.

4. Leverage Digital Whiteboards: Digital tools like Miro or Jamboard allow your team to collaborate visually, which can spark creativity in new ways. You can work together in real-time to map out ideas, draw diagrams, or create mood boards. These visual tools can help facilitate brainstorming and make the creative process feel more dynamic and interactive.

5. Encourage Breaks and Downtime: Creativity doesn't happen on demand. In fact, taking breaks is one of the best ways to recharge your creative batteries. Encourage your team to take time away from the screen to clear their minds. Some of the best ideas come when you're not trying so hard to be creative.

The key to creativity in a remote team is balance; creating a structured yet flexible environment that encourages collaboration without stifling individuality. When you build the right space for your team to communicate openly and share ideas, the magic happens.

Chapter 8
Technology Troubles

If there's one thing we've all learned in the remote work era, it's this: technology can make or break your day. A slow internet connection, a software glitch, or a video call that freezes right in the middle of an important discussion can leave you feeling frustrated and disconnected. The reality is, while remote work offers flexibility and freedom, it also comes with its own set of tech challenges. And let's face it, if the tech fails, everything else tends to fall apart.

In this chapter, we'll explore the common technology troubles remote workers face, from unreliable internet to software mishaps. We'll also go over some best practices for setting up your tech for success, and we'll dive into some essential cybersecurity basics to keep your work (and personal data) safe while working remotely.

Internet Reliability and Software Lags

The most frustrating tech issue for remote workers? Hands down, it's unreliable internet. Picture this: you're on an important Zoom call, your presentation is up, and then; Bam! The screen freezes, and you're suddenly talking to a bunch of blank squares. It's a nightmare, right? And it doesn't stop with video calls. A slow or unstable internet connection can make uploading files, sending emails, and even joining virtual meetings an exercise in patience.

However, it's not just the internet that can trip you up. Software lags and glitches are another pain point for remote workers. Whether it's the software you use to track projects or the cloud-based tools for team collaboration, dealing with slow-loading pages or random crashes is a huge productivity killer. It's a constant game of troubleshooting and rebooting, and when you're trying to work on a deadline, it can feel like the universe is conspiring against you.

So, how do you handle these common tech problems? It all comes down to preparation. Here are some tips:

Check Your Internet Speed:

First things first, make sure your internet connection is up to the task. Use speed-testing tools like Speedtest to measure your download and upload speeds. If your internet is consistently slow, consider upgrading your plan or switching providers. Many video conferencing tools (like Zoom) recommend speeds of at least 3 Mbps for HD video calls, so keep that in mind when testing.

Have a Backup Plan:

Tech issues are unpredictable, so always have a backup. If your internet goes out, consider using your phone's hotspot as a temporary fix. Make sure all essential files are stored on the cloud or external hard drive so you can access them even if something goes wrong with your primary device.

Update Software Regularly:

Regularly updating your software, whether it's your operating system, apps, or security software, helps prevent bugs and glitches. These updates often fix known issues, improve performance, and ensure compatibility with the latest tools. It might seem like a hassle, but it's worth it to keep everything running smoothly.

Best Practices for a Smooth Tech Setup

Your tech setup is your foundation for success as a remote worker. Having the right equipment and setting it up properly can save you a lot of frustration and time. Here's what you need to do to ensure your tech is working for you, not against you:

1. Choose the Right Hardware: Start with a reliable laptop or desktop. Invest in a computer with enough RAM and processing power to handle your tasks, nothing is worse than a computer that lags when you're multitasking. Depending on your work, a larger monitor or even a dual monitor setup can make a world of difference.

2. High-Quality Audio and Video: Clear communication is vital in remote work. If you're on video calls regularly, invest in a good webcam and microphone. External mics often have better sound quality than built-in laptop mics. Likewise, a good quality webcam can make you look more professional and help others focus on the content of your call, rather than the pixelated blur of your face.

3. Stable Wi-Fi Router: The internet doesn't just depend on your internet service provider; it also relies on the quality of your Wi-Fi router. If you're working from a different room than your router, or if your connection is unstable, consider upgrading to a more powerful router or setting up a mesh system to extend coverage across your home.

4. Organize Your Workspace: A smooth tech setup isn't just about the tools, it's about how you organize them. Keep your workspace tidy, with all cables neatly arranged to avoid tangling or tripping over them. You'll want easy access to your keyboard, mouse, and monitor, without any distractions.

5. Use a Surge Protector: Power surges can destroy sensitive electronics. Protect your devices with a good surge protector, especially if you live in an area prone to power outages or storms.

Cybersecurity Basics for Remote Work

Working remotely means more than just adjusting to a different work environment, it also means taking extra precautions to protect your data. Remote work comes with its own set of cybersecurity risks, from potential hacking attempts to phishing scams. But don't worry, a little awareness and the right tools can go a long way in keeping you safe. So:

1. Use Strong, Unique Passwords: This is one of the easiest ways to secure your accounts. Avoid using simple, easily guessable passwords like "password123" or "qwerty." Instead, create strong passwords with a mix of upper and lowercase letters, numbers, and special characters. A password manager like LastPass or 1Password can help you generate and store complex passwords for all your accounts.

2. Enable Two-Factor Authentication: Two-factor authentication (2FA) adds an extra layer of security by requiring a second form of verification, usually a code sent to your phone or email, before granting access to your account. It's an easy step to set up and can significantly improve your cybersecurity.

3. Avoid Public Wi-Fi for Sensitive Work: Public Wi-Fi networks (like the ones at coffee shops or airports) are convenient, but they're also prime targets for hackers. Avoid using public Wi-Fi for sensitive work like logging into your bank account or sending confidential business documents. If you must use public Wi-Fi, make sure to use a VPN (Virtual Private Network) to encrypt your connection.

4. Keep Software Updated: As we mentioned earlier, keeping your software up to date isn't just about performance, it's also about security. Many updates include patches that protect against new vulnerabilities, so make sure your antivirus software, operating system, and apps are all regularly updated.

5. Be Cautious with Phishing Attempts: Phishing is one of the most common ways hackers steal information. If you receive an unsolicited email asking for sensitive information, don't click on any links or download attachments. Always verify the sender's email address and be wary of any messages that sound too good to be true.

By setting up a reliable tech environment and practicing good cybersecurity hygiene, you'll be able to focus on your work instead of constantly battling technology issues. The right setup can make your remote work experience smoother, more productive, and, most importantly, secure.

Chapter 9
Building Remote Resilience

In this chapter, we'll look at daily routines that can help strengthen your resilience, strategies for staying socially connected even when you're physically alone, and ways to prevent burnout before it creeps in and derails your well-being.

Daily Routines That Strengthen Mental Toughness

Resilience isn't something you're born with; it's something you build over time. And much like physical fitness, it requires regular practice. When you work remotely, your routine becomes your anchor. It's what keeps you grounded, focused, and able to handle the ups and downs of remote work. Therefore:

1. Start Your Day with Purpose: One of the biggest challenges of remote work is the temptation to roll out of bed and dive straight into your laptop. But skipping a morning routine can leave you feeling scattered and unprepared. Instead, start your day with a routine that sets you up for success. This could be a 10-minute meditation session, a quick workout, or even a cup of coffee while you read or plan your day. Creating a morning ritual not only sets the tone for your day, it also gives you something to look forward to.

2. Prioritize Physical Movement: Sitting at a desk all day can wear you down physically and mentally. To build resilience, make time for physical movement throughout your day. Whether it's a short walk, some light stretching, or a full-on workout, getting your body moving can help release stress, improve your mood, and boost productivity. Research by the American Psychological Association shows that exercise is a great way to build mental toughness, it improves your overall well-being and helps you manage stress more effectively.

3. Set Clear Goals and Focus on Progress: One of the most powerful ways to build resilience is to break down big tasks into manageable steps. When you work remotely, it's easy to feel overwhelmed by the number of tasks on your plate. But instead of letting it all pile up, set clear daily goals for yourself. These don't have to be big goals; small, actionable tasks can give you a sense of accomplishment and keep you moving forward.

4. Practice Mindfulness: Remote work can be a whirlwind of meetings, emails, and tasks. Without proper mental boundaries, you can easily become overwhelmed. Practicing mindfulness, whether it's through meditation, journaling, or simply being present in the moment, can help you regain focus and reduce anxiety. Studies have shown that mindfulness reduces stress and increases emotional resilience, making it a crucial practice for remote workers.

Staying Socially Connected While Working Solo

One of the hardest parts of remote work is the loneliness that can creep in. When you're working from home, there's no one around to chat with, no one to grab lunch with, and no impromptu social breaks that often happen in an office setting. This isolation can quickly lead to feelings of disconnection and burnout. So, how do you stay socially connected when your coworkers aren't physically nearby? It's all about intentional connection:

1. Schedule Regular Check-ins: Don't wait for "organic" conversations to happen; schedule regular check-ins with colleagues, whether it's for work or just to catch up. These check-ins don't have to be formal meetings. Set up a weekly virtual coffee break or a monthly "team lunch" via video chat. These moments help maintain relationships and give you the social interaction you crave.

2. Join Virtual Communities: Look for online communities of remote workers in your field or related interests. Whether it's a Slack group, a LinkedIn community, or a virtual networking event, connecting with others who understand your experiences can be incredibly validating. It's not just about professional networking, it's about finding a support system of people who "get it."

3. Keep in Touch with Friends and Family: Remote work doesn't just isolate you from your coworkers, it can also put distance between you and your friends and family. Make an effort to maintain those personal relationships, whether it's through regular phone calls, video chats, or in-person meetups when possible. Social connections outside of work can help balance out the isolation of remote work.

Preventing Burnout Before It Starts

Burnout is a real threat for remote workers. The lines between work and personal life blur, and before you know it, you're working longer hours and feeling drained all the time. But burnout doesn't have to be inevitable. By being proactive and taking care of your mental and physical health, you can prevent it before it starts. Thus:

1. Set Clear Boundaries: One of the most effective ways to prevent burnout is to establish strong boundaries between your work life and personal life. Set clear start and end times for your workday, and stick to them. Create a designated workspace that you leave at the end of the day, literally walk away from your "office" and give yourself permission to unwind.

2. Take Regular Breaks: It's easy to keep working when you're at home, but working non-stop can quickly lead to burnout. Incorporate regular breaks into your day, whether it's a short walk, a coffee break, or just stepping away from your desk for a few minutes. Studies show that taking breaks improves productivity and prevents mental fatigue.

3. Prioritize Self-Care: It's easy to forget about self-care when you're busy juggling work and life, but it's essential for long-term resilience. Whether it's getting enough sleep, eating nourishing meals, or taking time for activities you enjoy, make sure to prioritize your well-being. The healthier you are physically and mentally, the better equipped you'll be to handle the challenges of remote work.

4. Seek Support: If you're feeling overwhelmed, don't be afraid to seek support. Talk to your manager, reach out to a friend or therapist, or join a peer support group. It's okay to not have all the answers, and asking for help when you need it is an important step in preventing burnout.

Building resilience as a remote worker is a process, it takes time and consistent effort. By creating routines that support your mental toughness, staying socially connected, and taking proactive steps to prevent burnout, you'll not only survive remote work, you'll thrive in it.

Chapter 10
The Future of Remote Work

The world of remote work is still evolving, and it's clear that this shift is not just a temporary phase. Whether it's the flexibility of working from anywhere or the ability to attract talent from across the globe, the future of remote work is looking bright. But it's not just about working from home anymore, it's about where you work and how you work. The lines between work and life will continue to blur, and new models, like hybrid work and digital nomadism, are becoming more popular. So, what does the future of remote work really look like, and how can you prepare for it?

In this chapter, we'll explore the rise of hybrid work models, the growing trend of digital nomadism, what successful remote companies are doing differently, and how you can create a sustainable remote work lifestyle that works for you.

Hybrid Models and Digital Nomadism

Hybrid work models have been gaining traction in recent years, and the pandemic only accelerated this trend. The hybrid model allows employees to work both in-office and remotely, giving them the flexibility to choose where they work based on their tasks, personal preferences, or even their mood.

Many companies are adopting hybrid work because it combines the benefits of remote work (like flexibility and autonomy) with the benefits of in-person collaboration (like team bonding and spontaneous creativity). According to a Gartner survey, 82% of company leaders plan to allow employees to work remotely some of the time. Hybrid models help companies strike a balance between flexibility and team cohesion, fostering a dynamic work environment that can adapt to changing needs.

What about digital nomadism? The idea of working remotely while traveling the world has gone from being a dream of freelancers to an attainable lifestyle for many full-time employees. Digital nomads are people who use technology to work from anywhere, be it a beach in Bali, a café in Paris, or a co-working space in Mexico City.

With the rise of remote work, digital nomadism has become a viable option for a growing number of professionals. There are even countries offering "*digital nomad visas*" that allow remote workers to live and work there for extended periods. For those who value travel and adventure, the digital nomad lifestyle offers the freedom to explore new places while continuing to build a career.

What Successful Remote Companies Do Differently

Not all remote companies are created equal. Some manage to make remote work truly successful, while others struggle to maintain productivity and morale. So, what sets the successful ones apart?

1. Strong Communication Practices: Remote companies that thrive tend to have clear communication channels and expectations. They use the right tools to stay connected—whether it's through instant messaging apps like Slack, video conferencing tools like Zoom, or project management software like Asana or Trello. They also prioritize regular check-ins and encourage open communication, so team members feel connected even when they're not in the same room.

2. Focus on Results, Not Hours: Successful remote companies focus on the outcomes their employees produce rather than the number of hours spent at the desk. This approach fosters a results-driven culture where employees are trusted to manage their own time and work in the way that suits them best.

3. Fostering a Strong Company Culture: Remote work can make it difficult to establish a sense of company culture, but successful remote companies put a lot of effort into building strong, inclusive cultures. They invest in team-building activities (virtual happy hours, online games, and team challenges) and make sure that new employees feel welcome, even from a distance.

4. Flexibility and Autonomy: Offering flexibility is a key factor in remote work success. Great remote companies trust their employees to get the work done, whether it's during traditional working hours or at 10 PM. They understand that life happens; children might need to be taken care of, errands need to be run, or personal projects require attention, and they provide the autonomy to balance personal and professional responsibilities.

5. Providing Resources for Success: Successful remote companies equip their employees with the tools and resources they need to succeed. From providing a budget for a home office setup to offering access to mental health resources or remote work training, these companies invest in their employees' well-being and productivity.

Creating a Sustainable Remote Work Lifestyle

The future of remote work will be a mix of flexibility, innovation, and self-management. But in order to thrive in this new world of work, it's essential to create a remote work lifestyle that's sustainable for the long haul. Therefore:

1. Set Boundaries: While remote work offers freedom, it can also blur the lines between your personal life and your work life. To create a sustainable lifestyle, it's essential to establish clear boundaries. Set specific work hours and stick to them. Create a designated workspace to physically separate your work from your personal life.

2. Prioritize Well-Being: Sustainability isn't just about work, it's about well-being. Make sure to prioritize self-care, physical health, and mental wellness. Set aside time for exercise, relaxation, hobbies, and social connection. Taking care of your mind and body is crucial to maintaining long-term productivity and happiness.

3. Embrace Continuous Learning: The remote work landscape is always evolving, and to keep up, you need to stay adaptable. Embrace opportunities to learn new skills, whether it's through online courses, reading, or networking with other professionals. Staying curious and open to change will help you stay competitive and resilient in the future of work.

4. Invest in Tech and Tools: Technology is the backbone of remote work. Make sure you have the tools, equipment, and software to work efficiently and securely. Stay updated on the latest remote work technologies that can improve your productivity, collaboration, and communication.

5. Maintain Flexibility: The beauty of remote work lies in its flexibility, and it's important to maintain that flexibility as the work landscape changes. Be open to adjusting your routine, workspace, or even the way you work to keep things fresh and to avoid burnout. Flexibility is key to making remote work sustainable in the long term.

The future of remote work is full of exciting possibilities. Hybrid models, digital nomadism, and the rise of fully remote companies are all paving the way for a more flexible, creative, and global workforce. But it's up to you to create a sustainable lifestyle that supports your well-being, work, and personal life. With the right mindset, tools, and strategies, you can build a remote work lifestyle that works for you now and in the future.

Conclusion

As we reach the end of our journey through the world of remote work, it's clear that this shift is more than just a trend, it's a transformation in how we think about work, collaboration, and personal well-being. The flexibility, freedom, and possibilities that remote work offers are unparalleled. But as we've discussed, it's not without its complexities. The challenges of isolation, blurred boundaries, and constant digital misfires are very real.

Still, what makes remote work truly remarkable is its potential for balance. When approached with intention, remote work allows us to craft a work-life experience that aligns with our personal goals, values, and rhythms. It offers a unique opportunity to work smarter, not harder, to reconnect with the things that matter most, and to define what productivity looks like on our terms.

The key is resilience. Just like in any other environment, remote work demands adaptability, discipline, and self-awareness. The tools, strategies, and habits we've explored throughout this book are designed to help you build that resilience, to tackle the challenges while embracing the incredible benefits that come with working from home (or anywhere, for that matter).

Whether you're a remote veteran or someone just starting out, remember: You have the power to shape your remote work life. Find your rhythm, set boundaries, stay connected, and keep evolving. With the right mindset and the right tools, you can thrive in this new world of work. The future is remote, let's make the most of it.

DARREN MASONE

References

Buffer. (2023). State of remote work 2023 report. https://buffer.com/state-of-remote-work/2023

Gallup, Inc. (2022). The future of hybrid work: 2022 survey results. https://www.gallup.com/workplace/390632/future-hybrid-work-2022.aspx

Stanford University. (2023). The productivity pitfalls of working from home in the COVID-19 era. Stanford Institute for Economic Policy Research.

Harvard Business Review. (2022). The loneliness of the hybrid worker.

Microsoft. (2022). Work trend index: Annual report. https://www.microsoft.com/en-us/worklab/work-trend-index

World Health Organization. (2022). Mental health at work. https://www.who.int/news-room/fact-sheets/detail/mental-health-at-work

Pew Research Center. (2023). How the pandemic changed work and commuting patterns.

Journal of Applied Psychology. (2021). Work-from-home productivity during the COVID-19 pandemic [Special issue]. 106(9), 1234-1268. https://doi.org/10.1037/apl0000893

American Psychological Association. (2022). Stress in America™: Work and well-being survey. https://www.apa.org/news/press/releases/stress/2022/work-well-being

Journal of Occupational Health Psychology. (2023). The paradox of remote work: Increased hours but decreased output. 28(1), 45-62. https://doi.org/10.1037/ocp0000331

National Bureau of Economic Research. (2022). Why working from home will stick (Working Paper No. 28731). https://www.nber.org/papers/w28731

Frontiers in Psychology. (2023). Zoom fatigue: A systematic review. 14, 1123456.

Deloitte Insights. (2023). The hybrid work model: Challenges and opportunities. https://www2.deloitte.com/us/en/insights/focus/human-capital-trends.html

McKinsey & Company. (2023). Americans are embracing flexible work - and they want more of it. https://www.mckinsey.com/industries/real-estate/our-insights/americans-are-embracing-flexible-work-and-they-want-more-of-it

Journal of Business and Psychology. (2022). Remote work and employee well-being: A meta-analysis. 37(4), 789-812. https://doi.org/10.1007/s10869-021-09767-y

www.ingramcontent.com/pod-product-compliance
Lightning Source LLC
Chambersburg PA
CBHW050728010526
44107CB00009B/776